Looe – An Introduct

Looe is a small fishing town in South East Cornwall. It is a popular venue for holiday makers, many of whom come from overseas to see the old houses, narrow streets and quaint charm of the old town.

Seagoing vessels of many types were built in Looe, a tradition which continues to this day but to a lesser degree, and the sea has always shaped the lives of those who lived there. Looe is in fact two towns, East and West Looe, with a tidal river flowing between, spanned by a stone bridge of seven, previously eight, arches. The present structure replaces an earlier bridge which was situated approximately twenty-five yards further downstream.

The towns were originally Rotten Boroughs, for almost three hundred years each returning two representatives to the House of Commons, indicating their importance in earlier times.

The original settlement was at Shutta, about half a mile up river. This was not visible from the sea, and so afforded some protection from marauding Corsairs based in Morocco and along the Sallee coast, who came capturing men to hold for ransom or sell into slavery.

Looe has produced some notable personages in the past and many less worthy citizens, mostly smugglers, who were a thorn in the side of the Revenue men. The long stone building at West Looe known locally as the "Coastguards", and easily recognisable by its central archway, is believed to have been the married quarters for the Preventative Officers.

The Old Guild Hall in East Looe still stands. It is now a museum, and reveals much about the town's interesting history. It is still possible to see through the hoards of visitors and gift shops to the essential charm of the town, and to imagine it peopled, as it had been for centuries, by merchants, seamen, smugglers and Preventative men. At one time a young boy called Robert Colliver roamed the streets. He left Looe to become an infamous pirate, but who knows what ghosts linger in the alleyways and dark corners? One perhaps with a cutlass in his hand!

It is Robert Colliver who is the subject of this book, not by any means Looe's most honourable citizen, but one whose infamy should at least be recorded, and who should be given his place in history.

The Authors

Robert Colliver

Looe's Arch Pirate

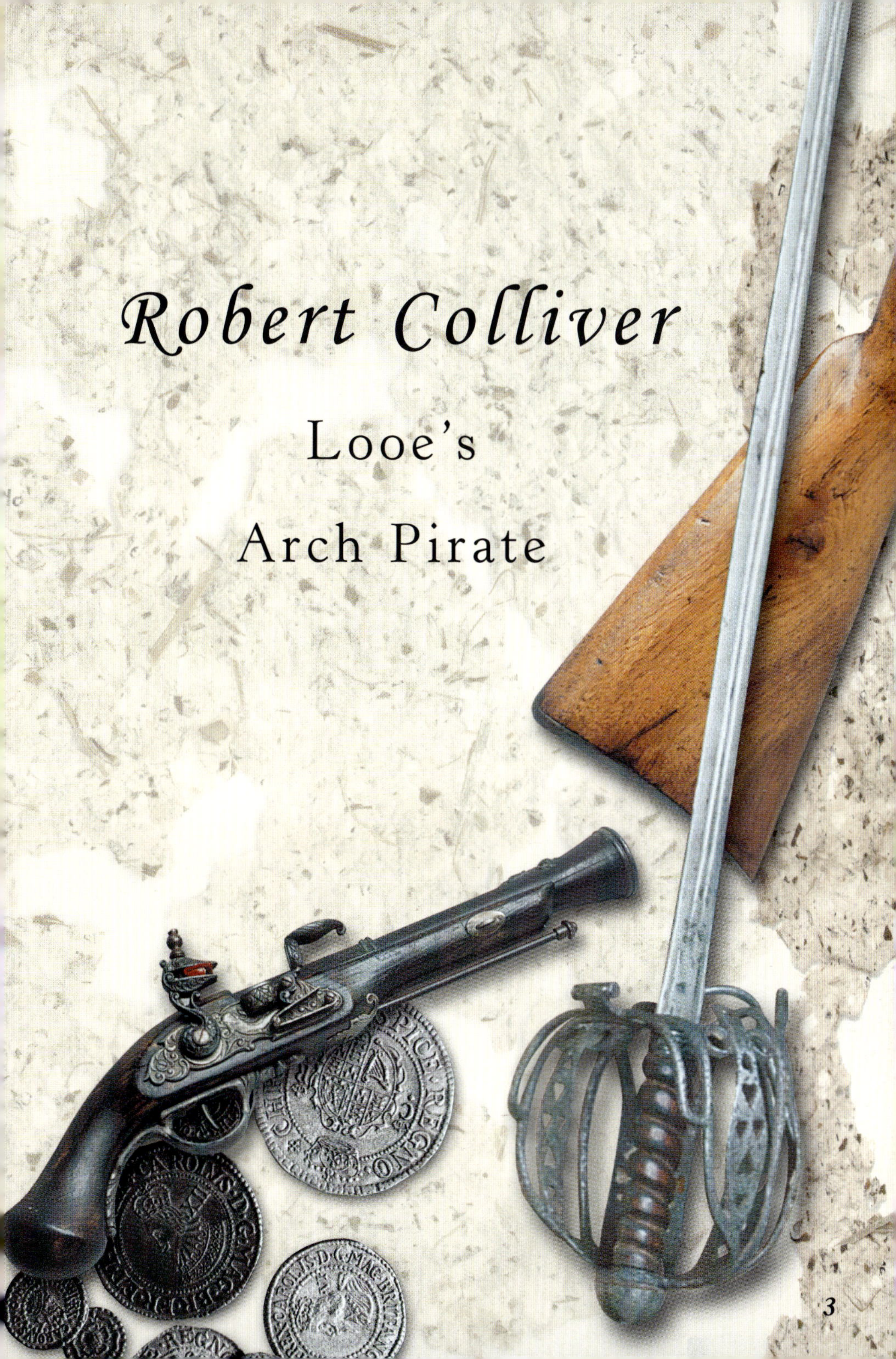

Septemb Thomas Heller & Margeret Trefry married
Octob John Welshman & Mary Spurre married
Octob Thomas ffretty & Joane Moyle married
October Pascho Colliver & Amue Kingwell married
October Thomas Colling & Ame Devonsheere married
Octo Edward Hore & Mariory Carre married
Nobember Edward Pope & Joane Nute married
January Henry Chill & Edith Diggins married

The record of the marriage of Pascho and Agnes Colliver. © Cornwall Record Office, Truro.

St. Martin's Church, East Looe.

"Robert Culliford, arch pirate." This is how a man born at East Looe was described at the trial of the famous Captain Kidd, and had it not been for the Cornishman's interference in Kidd's life the more famous but far less evil pirate might never have been hung!

Although all modern accounts give Robert the surname Culliford, trial records, correspondence about him, the name on his baptismal record and a letter signed by him all make it clear that his actual name was Colliver or Collover, but since standard spellings had not been established at that time other variations do occur. Colliver was born in East Looe in March 1666, the son of Pascho and Agnes Colliver. On his baptismal record his mother's name is given as Anne, a common diminutive of Agnes, but we have entries of her name in other registers, and her identity can therefore be established.

We know little about the Colliver family, but there are things which can

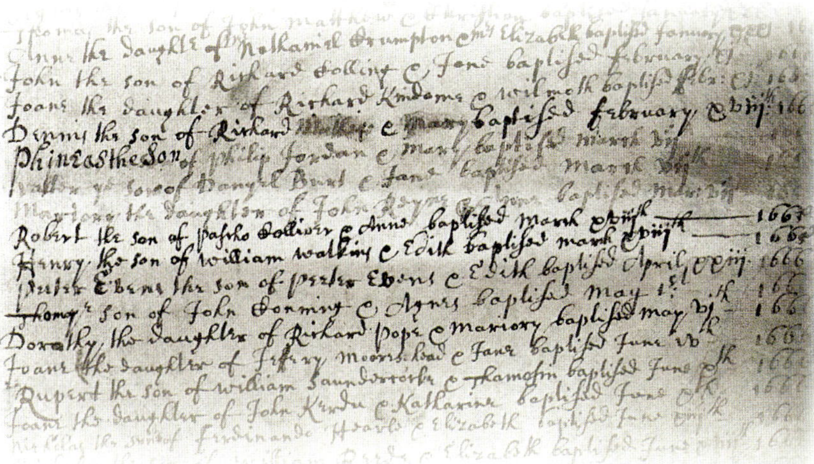
John the son of Richard [illegible] & Jone baptised Febr: [illegible]
Joane the daughter of Richard [illegible] & Wilmoth baptised February [illegible]
Denny the son of Richard [illegible] & Mary baptised March [illegible]
Phineas the Son of Philip Jordan & Mary baptised March [illegible]
Robert the son of Pascho Colliver & Anne baptised March [illegible] 1665
Henry the son of William Walkins & Edith baptised March [illegible] 1665
Peter Evens the son of Peter Evens & Edith baptised April [illegible] 1666
Thomas the son of John [illegible] & Agnes baptised May 1st 1666
Dorothy the daughter of Richard Pope & Mariory baptised May [illegible] 1666
Joane the daughter of [illegible] & Jane baptised June [illegible] 1666
Rupert the son of William [illegible] & [illegible] baptised June [illegible] 1666
Joane the daughter of John [illegible] & Katharine baptised June [illegible] 1666

The Baptismal record of Robert Colliver at St. Martin's Church, East Looe. © Cornwall Record Office, Truro.

be safely assumed. They were not of the gentry, they held no large estates, nor did they marry into any of the locally established great families, but in 1633 we find a record of a certain Philip Colliver, probably a relation of Robert, who was a church warden, a position of considerable social

standing in those days, and Robert himself could read and write, suggesting some degree of affluence on the part of his parents, since education was not then the rule for the poorer people; yet when Robert entered service on a ship, it was not as an officer, as was normal for anyone well born. Considering that Looe was a busy and important port, it is possible that the Collivers were a merchant family, involved in some way with shipping.

Nothing is known of Robert Colliver's early life, but he appears in the records in 1690 on board a privateer brigantine, the Blessed William, captained by William Kidd. A privateer was an armed vessel owned and officered by a private person holding a commission from the government, and authorized to use it against hostile nations especially in the capture of merchant ships, and to take pirate vessels of any nation.

The Blessed William had twenty guns, and a crew of from eighty to ninety men who objected to Kidd's "ill treatment" of them. Kidd had killed one of his crew by hitting him over the head with a bucket. Infuriated by the bad treatment, and tempted by the £2,000 booty in the hold of the ship, the crew led by Colliver and two other men, Burgess and Mason, mutinied on February 2nd, and captured the ship while Kidd was on shore. This was the first but not the last encounter where Colliver bested Captain Kidd, later to become infamous in his own right.

Leaving Kidd stranded, the crew of the Blessed William, captained by Mason, sailed to New York for a refit. They arrived some time in May 1690, the crew selling the cargo and slaves. They then accepted a commission from Leisler, a merchant and captain of the militia, to attack shipping in the Gulf of St Lawrence. They took six ships one of which appears to have been named the Pearl later renamed the Jacob. Since this was a better ship the crew transferred to it, selling the Blessed William. It was the custom to rename captured ships, and the records can cause confusion when the same vessel in varying accounts may be given two or even three different names when a single event is being reported. The prizes taken by the Jacob were condemned by the court, so the crew had a legal right to them. She set sail for the Indian Ocean at the end of December 1690.

On the new ship, Colliver filled the post of quartermaster, and it is known that the Pearl/Jacob sailed to Mangalore where Colliver, Mason and some others were left ashore in 1694. The reason is not given, but it may have been that Colliver's homosexual activities were unacceptable to the rest of the crew.

Colliver then spent the next few years as a gunner's mate at Fort St George, Madras, but he again emerges as a pirate when he leads the crew of the ketch Josiah

in a mutiny, having taken her while she was at anchor in June 1696. She sailed to Anjego harbour, where her crew plundered and burnt the sloop Gingal, belonging to the East India Company, the very company that had employed Colliver previously. The pirates then sailed to the Nicobars, plundering, burning villages, slaughtering natives, and generally acting in a way far removed from the swash-buckling heroes of Hollywood and romantic novels. Colliver was at all times a cruel and brutal man, without compassion.

All did not go well for the pirates, for the Josiah was repossessed by James Croft who had been the armourer at Fort St George, and had come aboard with Colliver. Colliver himself was at the time of the recapture Iying drunk in his cabin with another man. They were overpowered and taken back to Madras for trial, but escaped death by benefit of the clergy, this being exemption from trial by secular court, and later from sentence for first convictions, enjoyed by all who could read. Colliver's education saved his life!

Oddly enough he was allowed to rejoin the East India Company, in spite of which, for a third time, he turned to piracy. This was probably because life on board ship was so harsh that piracy was considered an acceptable alternative. Conditions on board a pirate vessel were just as bad, but officers were elected not appointed, and the rewards were considerably greater. We next hear of Colliver on board the frigate Mocha which was renamed the Resolution. It was in this vessel that his reputation grew, and his acts of piracy increased. The Mocha/Resolution was at first captained by Ralph Stout, and along with another vessel called the Charming Mary (also called the Soldado) many crimes were now committed.

On February 15th 1697 the pirates took a large ship, the Alamshay, sailing from Surat to Bengal. It had an European crew who fought well, but lost eight men including the captain before surrendering to the pirates. The ship was plundered of her cargo and guns, but beyond this there was no unusual cruelty. The next vessel was not so lucky. A ship bound from Surat to Manilla was not only ransacked, after three pirates had been killed in the fight, but the passengers and crew who survived the attack were battened down in the hatches, and the pirates set fire to the ship, burning all on board to death.

The two pirate ships now decided to sail to the Maldives for careening (hauling out on their sides on the beach for cleaning the hull, and repairs) before taking a Portuguese ship on 29th March. On April 8th another

Surat ship became their victim. Again the ship was plundered, and this time they took captive sixteen Lascars to help crew their own undermanned ships. They also abducted the native pilot, believing him to be useful to them.

Shortly after the 8th April 1697, the Resolution parted company with the Charming Mary, and sailed to the Maldives for a refit. While there, Ralph Stout was murdered by his own company whilst ashore on a watering expedition, and the quartermaster, Robert Colliver, was elected to be the new captain. It was at some time in this period that Colliver seems to have formed a homosexual relationship with his "great consort", John Swann.

It was on July 7th 1697, while under the captaincy of Colliver, that the Resolution was beaten in an encounter with the East India Company ship, the Dorrill. Accounts of the incident survive, interestingly from one man on the Dorrill, and another on board the Resolution.

The first of these accounts is that of William Reynolds.

(William Reynolds, Supercargo)—"To Sir John Gayer

"A Large (full) Account of the Action of the Ship Dorrill with the Pirate Ship Mocha, dated Achin, 28th August 1697.

"Most Respected and Right Honourable Sir,

"These presents truly representeth a scheme of what misfortune befell us as we were going through the Straits of Mallacca in pursuance of our pretended voyage. Vizt, Wednesday the 7th July at 5 o'clock in the morning we espied a ship to windward; as soon as it was well light, we persèved her to bear down upon us. We thought at first she had been a Dutchman, bound for Achin or Bengall untill wee persèved she had taken down all her galleries, and did then suppose her to be what to our dreadful sorrow we afterwards found her. Wee got our shipp into the best posture of defence that such sudden emergent necessity would permitt of, and kept looking out expecting to see an Island called Pulo Verello, but as then, saw it not. About eight of the clock the shipp came fairly within shott.

"Then wee saw that in room of her galleries there were large sally ports in each of which was a large gun, seemingly of brass. Her taffrail was likewise taken down. Wee, having done what wee possibly

could do to prepare ourselves, fearing wee might suddenlie bee sett upon sent all our people to their respective quarters for action, and now hoisted our collours whiche the Captain desired nailed to the staffe in sighte of the enemy; which was immediately done. As soon as they perceived oure collours, they hoisted theirs which were the Union Jack, and let fly a Broad Red Pendant, at their masthead.

"The Pirate being now in little more than half pistol shott, wee colde discerne abundance of men whiche went forward to the quarter deck as wee supposed, to consult. They stood as wee stood but wee spoke neither to the other. At noone it fell so calme that wee were afraid that wee shoulde by the sea, bee hove one on the other. At noone sprung up a gale. The Pirate kept as we kept (sailing parallel). At three o'clocke the Pirate backt her saile and they went from us. Wee kept close hauled, the wind beeing contrary for Mallacca. When about seven miles distant from us the Pirate tacked and again stood after us with all sail.

"At Six in the evening wee saw the lookt for Island at whiche time the Pirate came up on oure starboard side within shott. Wee saw that he kept a man at each topmast head looking out till it was dark then he hauled off a little from us, though keeping company all night. Att eight in the morning he drewe neare us by whiche time wee had brought up oure other four guns that were in the hold, and were now the best posture of defence wee coulde desire. Hee drawing nere to us and seeing thatt if we woulde wee colde nott get from him, hee far outsailing us bye and large, oure Captain resolved to see what the Rogue woulde do, so ordered us to hand oure small sailes, and furl oure mainsail.

"Hee, seeing this, did the like, and as wee came back to him, beat his drum and sounded his trumpetts, and then haled us foure times before wee woulde answer him. At last it was thought fitting to see what he woulde say, soe the Boatswaine spoke to him as ordered whiche was thatt wee came from London. Then he enquired, was it peace or war with France. We answered thatt itt was universal peace throughout Europe at which he pawsed a little, and then answered 'That's well.' He further enquired had wee touched at Achin; we said a boate came off, but came not neare us by seven miles. Further he enquired oure Captain's name and whither bound. We answered to Mallacca to which they replied, they also, and would oure Captain come aboard for a glass of wine?

"Wee declining, said they 'Shall meete you at Mallacca.' Then again he called to us to lie bye and he woulde come aboard us. Our answer was 'Too late.' He said 'True, it is late for China' and enquired whether wee should touch at the Water Islands (Pulo Ondan) for water. Wee said wee shoulde. Then saide hee 'So shall wee.' After he had asked us all these questions wee desired to know who hee was and whence hee came. Hee saide from London, theire Captain's name Collyford, the ship the Resolution, bound for China. Wee knew this Collyford had been Gunner's mate at Madras and run away with the Josiah Ketch. Thus passed the 8th July. Friday the 9th hee beeing some distance from us, wee coulde disceren a fellow on the Quarter deck wearing a sword.

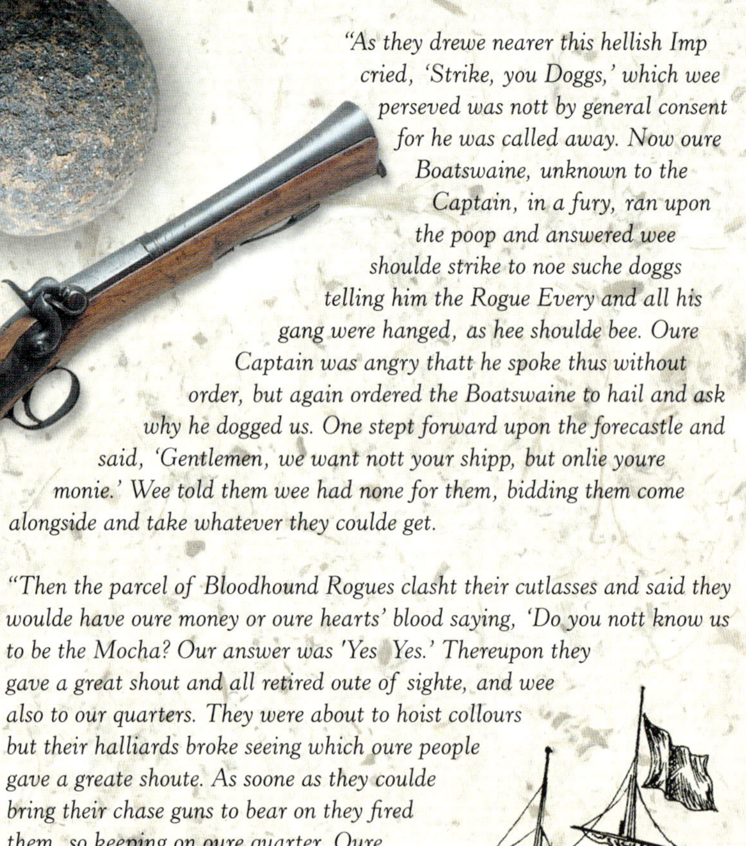

"As they drewe nearer this hellish Imp cried, 'Strike, you Doggs,' which wee persevd was nott by general consent for he was called away. Now oure Boatswaine, unknown to the Captain, in a fury, ran upon the poop and answered wee shoulde strike to noe suche doggs telling him the Rogue Every and all his gang were hanged, as hee shoulde bee. Oure Captain was angry thatt he spoke thus without order, but again ordered the Boatswaine to hail and ask why he dogged us. One stept forward upon the forecastle and said, 'Gentlemen, we want nott your shipp, but onlie youre monie.' Wee told them wee had none for them, bidding them come alongside and take whatever they coulde get.

"Then the parcel of Bloodhound Rogues clasht their cutlasses and said they woulde have oure money or oure hearts' blood saying, 'Do you nott know us to be the Mocha? Our answer was 'Yes Yes.' Thereupon they gave a great shout and all retired oute of sighte, and wee also to our quarters. They were about to hoist collours but their halliards broke seeing which oure people gave a greate shoute. As soone as they coulde bring their chase guns to bear on they fired them, so keeping on oure quarter. Oure guns could not bear for a short time, but as soon as did hap, we gave the Pirates better than they did like.

"His second shott caried away oure sprit sayle yard. About half an hour after or more he carried on and came alongside after which wee both continewed powering owre fire, wee giving sometimes

single guns, and sometimes broadsides of three or four, as opportunity presented, and could bring them to doe best service. He was going to lay us athwart the hawse, but by good fortune Captain Hide frustrated his attempt by powering in a broadside which made him give back and goe astarne where he lay without firing for a small space. Then he fired one gun which shot came through oure Roundhouse window though without damage.

"He now filled and bore away, and when about a quarter mile off fired another gun which wee answered. Aboute an houre after he tacked and came up with we making no sayle, but lying bye to wait him. The distance at most in all our firing was never more than two ships' lengths, the time of our engagement from half an hour after eleven till three in the afternoon. At this time he lay aloof and made no sign to renew the engagement. When wee came to see what damage we had sustained wee found our chiefe mate Mr. Smith wounded in the leg close up to the knee with a piece of chaine, and the barber's mate two fingers shott off as hee was sponging a gun.

"The Gunners' boy had his legg shott off when in the waist. Oure Quartermaster John Amos, had his leg shott off when att the helm, the Boatswaine's boy, a lad of thirteen, shott in the thigh going right through and splintering the bone, John Osbourne, in the Roundhouse, wounded in the temple, the Captain's boy on the Quarter deck, his skull raised by a shott. William Reynolds his boy, his hat shot off and his hand sore wounded, and John Blake, half his calf shott away.

"The shipps damage is the mizzen maste shott away in the cap ('twas a miracle it stood so long), all oure rigging save one rope only shott to pieces, our mainemast ten feet from the deck cutt eight inches deep by great shott, a great shot through the Roundhouse, one on the quarter deck,

two in the forecastle, two in the bread room, which cawsed us to make much water and damaged the greater part of our bread. They dismounted two of our guns in the stearidge, two in the waist, one in the Roundhouse and one in the forecastle with abundance more damage 'twould be tedious to relate. Their small shot was mostly tin and tutenagle (pewter) and they fired pieces of glass bottles, teapotts, chains, stones and what not, which we found on our decks.

"We persewed abundance of our great shott pass through the Rogue's sayles and our hope is to have done him such damage as will now make him shun any Europe ship. At night wee persewed and kept close to their lights, and in the morning they made off as far as wee coulde discerne. We knotted and spliced our rigging and in the morning made all haste to repair our damages. At the beginning our men seeing the Pirates stand after us wee coulde perseve their countenances to bee dejected. Wee chered them what wee coulde, and the Captain and wee, oute of our own proper money, gave to every man and boy three dollars each which animated them, and wee further promised them if wee took the Pirate ship for every prisoner, five pounds, besides a gratuity from oure Gentlemen employers.

"At 9 o'clock July 10th wee persewed the Rogue make from us, so gave the Almighty our most condign thanks that hee had delivered us from the worst of oure enemies, for, truly the Pirate was very strong having at least 100 Europeans aboarde, besides 10 patereroes and two small mortars in the forecastle head, his lower tier being, wee judged sixteen, and eighteen pounders. The 12th July, died the Boatswaine's boy, George Mopp, Friday the 16th, died the Gunner's boy, Thomas Matthews, Sunday the 18th, died the barber, Andrew Miller, Sunday the 25th, died the Chiefe mate, Mr. John Smith. The other two are yet in a deplorable condition and wee are ashore here to refresh ourselves. The Chinese report that these Rogues

careened at the Maldives, where they gave an end to their Commanding Rogue, Ralph Stout, who they murdered for attempting to run away."

The second account is that of William Willocks.

"A Narrative About the Mocha Frigatt, written by William Willocks, prisoner aboard her for eleven months."

"About the end of July, the Pyrates met with a Europe ship near to Pulo Verrero. They came right up with her and haled her. The ship's name I do not remember, but they gave her Commander, Captain Hide, newly arived from London. Hell was never in greater confusion than was then aboard the Pyrate, some being for fighting under French Collours, some for shewing no Collours and some for not fighting at all. The Captain laid down his charge, because of such confusion. Then 'bout ship they go to choose another Captain. All this time they were within speech of each other so that the other ship could hear what they said.

"At length they concluded to fight, and the Captain resumed his place again. Then they went after the Europe ship. They came close up to her weather quarter so they could call to her and were asked what they wanted. Said they 'Money we want, and money we shall have.' 'That's well,' said the English ship, 'Come and take it.' So the Pyrates gave three cheers and went to their quarters. First they fired their two chase guns into the English ship, but before they could fire again they received both her broadsides, he taking care to work his ship to the best advantage and having about 20 guns mounted and they as good as the Pyrate.

"They had not passed above three or four broadsides before I could see the Pyrates become disheartened. Said they 'Here we shall get nothing

but broken bones, and if we lose a mast, where shall we get another!' they having received a great shott right in the heart of the foremast going clean through. Says the Pyrate Captain, 'We have wind enough, let us go about ship and take him, for he lies by for us.' Says one, 'You may put her about yourself an you will, for I'll fight no more.' 'Nor I,' says another, which then became the general cry. So they let fall their mainsail and foresail, and stood away on their course, seeing which the English ship also set her sails and left them."

Even after the setback of this encounter, the Resolution still captured three ships before sailing to Cape Negrais in South Burma to be refitted, and to share out the booty. They made a temporary base there before sailing with a crew of about forty men to the Isle of St Marie off Madagascar, and to the next encounter with Captain Kidd,

Adventure Galley

one which led to tragedy for Kidd, culminating in his trial and execution.

Madagascar and the Isle of St. Marie, © Royal Geographical Society.

Colliver and his crew were already at anchor when on April 1st 1698 Captain Kidd sailed into harbour on board the Adventure Galley, along with the Ruparel, also known as either the Maiden or November, because she was captured in that month. A few days later on 6/7th April a prize ship of Kidd's arrived, called the Quedah Merchant, also called Adventure Prize. At this time Kidd was still officially a privateer, and supposed to capture pirates, in spite of his own more than questionable exploits with merchant shipping. There were many accounts given of the events that followed, depending on whether prosecution or defence was being pressed at Kidd's trial.

The truth is probably a mixture of both. Kidd was no innocent, being a harsh man with piratical experience himself, but he could have had little personal liking for Colliver, having already lost the Blessed William to him, and he was probably quite eager to capture the Cornishman, but circumstances prevented it.

When Kidd sailed into the harbour some of Colliver's men fled to the woods, suspecting that they were about to be taken. Others rowed out to meet the privateer, to discover Kidd's intentions. Kidd claimed that he ordered his men to capture the pirates, but that they refused, saying they would rather shoot Kidd himself. Kidd claimed that he barricaded himself in his cabin, piling bales of goods against the door, that he armed himself with pistols, ready to defend his ship, but that defence was impossible. If this were true, love of life soon made him change his attitude, and feign friendship with the 'arch pirate' Colliver. Being at the mercy of his own crew, who had defected to

Colliver and his pirates, Kidd put on an act of what must have been hypocritical amity and even jollity, going on board the Resolution, where, as it was claimed at Kidd's trial ... they made a tub of bomboo, as they call it, it is made of water, limes and sugar, and there they drank to one another; and says Captain Kidd *'Before I would do you any damage, I would rather my soul should broil in Hellfire'*. Kidd assured the pirates that he was *"...as bad as they,"*.

Kidd's actions temporarily saved his life and that of his brother-in-law who sailed with him, and meant that he kept a share of the booty, but also led to his trial and eventual hanging.

Between ninety-seven and one hundred of his men were now part of Colliver's gang, and to ensure his goodwill Kidd presented the Cornishman with four cannon from his own ship as a sign of friendship. In all probability, Colliver would have taken them anyway, but Kidd had his own life to consider, so the token was more politically wise than made from any genuine feeling. However, it all counted against Kidd at his eventual trial. Having had everything his own way, Colliver left St Marie about June 15th 1698 on the Mocha/Resolution, bound for Johanna, leaving Kidd with only twenty men, and the Adventure Galley, a ship so unseaworthy that she had to be pumped at all times. Colliver took the slaves who did the pumping with him, so Kidd had no means of leaving the island. He decided to scupper and burn the Adventure Galley the remaining wreckage of which was recently discovered by American divers.

The Resolution meanwhile had sailed with a crew of about one hundred and thirty men, and forty guns at her ports. For the second time the Cornishman had got the upper hand of Captain Kidd, who when he eventually returned to New York found himself arrested for piracy and sent to London for trial. It was within months of leaving the unfortunate Kidd at St Marie that Colliver and the Resolution again teamed up with Captain Chivers and the Charming Mary/Soldado, and claimed the biggest prize of his career, a 600 ton merchantman called the Great Mahomet, sailing in the Gulf of Khambhat. Ibrahim Khan, the owner of the vessel, was aboard, and he claimed that the action was fiercely fought on both sides. About twenty pirates were killed whilst over

three hundred of the passengers and crew of the Great Mahomet were either killed or thrown overboard. Ibrahim Khan further remarked:

"These dreadful villains tortured the Nakhoda, together with the merchants, and all whom they suspected of having hidden money or jewels, most cruelly. Not content with this even, when they had extracted a confession by such vile means they shot the poor wretches and threw them overboard, living or dead. They then put about 150 of the passengers into boats, without oars, sails or even water, and cast them off, keeping about sixty women aboard. Fortunately the wind and tide favoured those set adrift and they reached the shore in safety. The poor women who were kept on the ship were most barbarously treated by the Pirates in their usual manner. Some stabbed themselves to death and others threw themselves into the sea rather than endure the outrages they were subjected to".

A letter from Fort St George dated 3rd January 1699 gave the value of the cargo on the Great Mahomet as 25 lakhs of rupees, which when shared out between the pirates on the two marauding vessels came to approximately £800 per man. In April 1999, Colliver wrote the one letter that survives in his own handwriting. He was in St Marie and wrote to a Mrs Whaley in New York, "concarninge youer husbondes will" in which everything was left to her and her children, and would be delivered to her. With all the loot, together with that previously plundered from other ships, Colliver was a rich man, and there was no need to risk his life in further exploits. It was time for a change.

The year before, Thomas Warren and his squadron had been sent to the East Indies with three commissioners to receive the

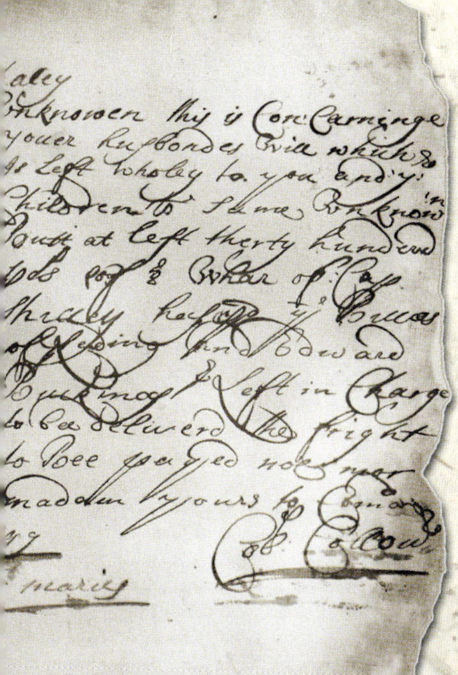
[illegible]aley
Unknowen this is Concarninge
youer husbondes will which he
as left wholey to you and y[illegible]
children to same unknown in
South at left therty hundered
[illegible]
[illegible]
[illegible]
[illegible]
[illegible] & Left in Charge
to be deliverd the fright
to bee [illegible]
madam yours to Command
[illegible] Collover
[illegible]marie

Robert Colliver's letter to Mrs Whaley

© Public Record Office, Kew.

14

[illegible]

Thomas Warren of London Marriner Voluntarily maketh Oath, That in the Month of January 169 8/9 he proceeded on a Voyage under ye Comand of Captn Thomas Warren Commadore and Commander in Chief of a Squadron of Men of Warr bound for the East Indies – In March 169 8/9 a Paper of Instructions in Writeing Signed by the said Commadore Warren, Izraell Hayes & Peter Delanoy Esqrs: his Maties Commissionrs, a True Copie whereof is hereunto annext was delivered to this Deponent, in pursuance whereof in the Month of August 1699 he arrived at the Island of St. Marie's near Madagascar in the East Indies in the Ship called the Vine Pink – That upon his first arrivall there one John Walker came on Board the sd Ship, to informe himselfe of the reasons of the said Voyage, which this Deponent discovered by giveing him an Account thereof, and about 1 of ye Clock of the same Day this Deponent sent one Henry Berkley ye Chirurgeon of this Deponents said Ship ashoar, to give notice of this Deponents arrivall & his Maties Proclamation; and the next Day one Robert Cullouer attended with Severall Negro Servants came on Board the sd Ship Vine Pink, And desired to see this Deponents said Instructions, and one of His Maties said Proclamations, which this Deponent Complyed with, apprehending the same to be his Duty, and Indorsed on the said Proclamation delivered to the said Robert Cullouer the time of his acceptance thereof, Signing the same with this Deponents Name, And this Deponent Saith that as Soon as he had Signed and delivered the said Proclamation, the said Robert Cullouer Expressed great Satisfaction and acknowledgements of his Maties Grace and Favour, and then gave this Deponent an Account of a great Number of Persons on the said Island of Madagascar with their Places of Settlements, Promiseing to prevaile on them to Submitt to his Matie and accept of Proclamations from this Deponent – And this Deponent Saith, that in a short time afterwards Seaventeen Persons Voluntarily applyed to this Deponent and accepted his Maties said Proclamations, this Deponent first Endorseing the time of the said Deliverie on Each of the said Proclamations, with this Deponents name thereon. And this Deponent further Saith, that he stayed at the said Island of St. Maries about two Months Expecting the said Squadron of Men of Warr and the said Commissionrs. But this Deponent is since informd, the said Commissionrs proceeded Directlie to India with Sr. William Norris

surrender of pirates in return for pardons. Warren deputized his son, also called Thomas, to go to Madagascar in August 1699 to deal in the name of the commissioners, and Warren Jnr. persuaded twenty-two pirates including Colliver to surrender. Warren later reported, *"....and the next day one Robert Cullouer attended with several Negro servants, and came on board the said ship, "Vine Pink" Colliver requested to see the instructions for pardon and "... as soon as he had signed and delivered the said proclamation, the said Robert Cullouer expressed great satisfaction".*

Although there was later some question over the validity of the pardon, having not been granted by the commissioners in person, and so leading to some of those 'pardoned' getting hung, Colliver's pardon was eventually declared valid by the Lords of the Admiralty because his case was 'peculiar', the 'peculiarity' being that he turned King's evidence against his fellow pirates and shipmates, resulting in the hanging of many of them. At the time of his surrender, Colliver and about fourteen of his men left St Marie on the Vine Pink, and on 20th September 1699 arrived in Cape Town where Captain Lowth of the Loyal Merchant demanded that the pirates be handed over to him. Warren however refused to part with the men, and eventually sailed the Vine Pink to St Helena where the pirates were picked up by a man-of-war and returned to England.

In spite of his pardon, Colliver still had to stand trial, and in May 1701 at the Old Bailey many pirates including Captain Kidd and Captain Robert Colliver were to learn their fate. Kidd had no doubt been guilty of piracy, and he had murdered one of his own crewmen, a certain William Moore, yet on the scale of evil deeds his were considerably less than those of Colliver. Kidd was a doomed man from the beginning, a political scapegoat who had been commissioned as a privateer by the previous Whig government that the new Tory leaders were eager to discredit. One of the charges made against Kidd was that he associated with Colliver, who was "... *esteemed an arch pirate, and known to be so, yet this Cpt. Kidd that was commissioned to take the pirates, instead of taking him, grows to an intimacy with him*". Ironically, the arch pirate himself was eventually freed!

Kidd was convicted and condemned to be hung. After his sentence he swore that *"I am the innocentist person of them all, only I have been sworn against by perjured persons"*. He was hung at Execution Dock, fortunately too drunk to be fully aware of what was happening, and his body was left to hang in chains.

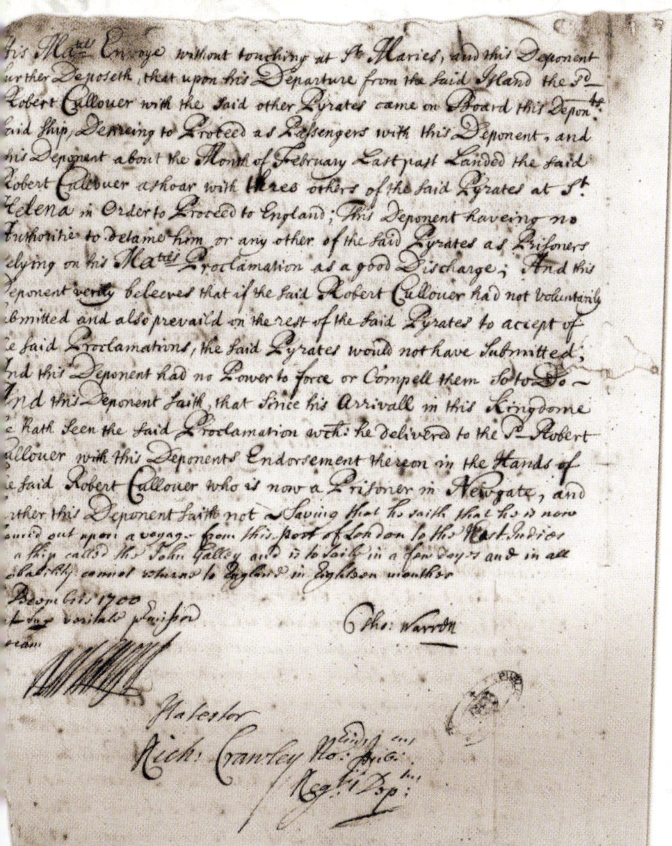
his Matie Envoye without touching at St. Maries, and this Deponent
urther Deposeth, that upon his Departure from the said Island the sd
Robert Callouer with the said other Pyrates came on Board this Depont
said Ship, Desireing to Proceed as Passengers with this Deponent, and
his Deponent about the Month of February Last past Landed the said
Robert Callouer ashoar with three others of the said Pyrates at St.
Helena in Order to Proceed to England; This Deponent haveing no
Authoritie to detaine him or any other of the said Pyrates as Prisoners
elying on his Maties Proclamation as a good Discharge; And this
Deponent verily beleeves that if the said Robert Callouer had not Voluntarily
ubmitted and also prevail'd on the rest of the said Pyrates to accept of
e said Proclamations, the said Pyrates would not have Submitted;
nd this Deponent had no Power to force or Compell them so to Do —
And this Deponent saith, that since his Arrivall in this Kingdome
e hath seen the said Proclamation wch he delivered to the sd Robert
allouer with this Deponents Endorsement thereon in the Hands of
e said Robert Callouer who is now a Prisoner in Newgate, and
urther this Deponent saith not Saving that he saith that he is now
[illegible] out upon a voyage from this port of London to the West Indies
a ship called the John Galley and is to saile in a few days and in all
[illegible] cannot returne to England in eighteen months

[illegible] 1700

Tho: Warren

Thomas Warren's Letters

In the meantime Colliver had a different ending, having turned Kings evidence. At the same session at the Old Bailey he was arraigned with some other pirates on many charges. For taking the ship Great Mahomet and seizing her goods he pleaded not guilty. For taking another unnamed ship he pleaded not guilty. For taking another Moorish ship he pleaded not guilty. These were clearly just specimen charges, in no way accounting for the whole of his piratical adventures, but when the trial started Colliver retracted his plea of innocence, and changed to one of guilty, whilst arguing that he came to court under the protection of a pardon.

Although he had been reprieved, Colliver was nevertheless returned to jail. The reason for his detention is made evident in a letter dated December 9th 1701. Thomas Bale wrote saying that there were several prisoners in Marshalsea who were to be tried shortly for piracy, *".... but in regards our most material witness against the chiefest of them, Cpt. Burgess, is Robert Collover, a prisoner in Newgate."* A reminder of Colliver's pardon is contained in the letter, and the information that he was *"....instrumental by his evidence of convicting those he knows to have been guilty of these crimes"*. The letter adds that there is *"no probability"* of convicting Burgess and others without Colliver's testimony. Bale also wrote that *"... by this man's (Colliver's) pardon we shall be able to make the proof appear more fully against them"*. An early date for the trial of Burgess was urged so that Colliver might be freed. Burgess, it will be remembered, was one of Colliver's friends who had conspired with him to take the Blessed William from Captain Kidd in his first piratical exploit. Loyalty was not a feature of Colliver's character.

On April 9th 1702 there was another letter from Thomas Bale requesting the release of the Cornishman, *"...the Queen..."* (Queen Anne had ascended to the throne in March 1702) *"...having been pleased to sign a warrant for the pardon of Cpt. Robert Collover"*, but with a question over the payment for the pardon. Bale argued that Colliver could not pay for his pardon while he was in jail, *"...his friends having nothing to do with him as long as he continues in prison"*. Bale made a strong case that *"...the making of a special pardon is for the public*

service in order to his being specially made a legal witness against criminals, his Excellency won't be pleased to command me to supply the charge which by his present indigent circumstances I humbly believe he is not able to pay."

Colliver was released and fades from the records. He may have pleaded indigent circumstances while in jail, but there was no mention of the thousands of pounds that he had looted in acts of piracy over the years. We do not know if any or all of it was confiscated, but it seems unlikely that Colliver would have surrendered and given up a fortune just to be on the right side of the law. He had never shown any regard for either the law or common decency in his life of violence and cruelty. We have no record of his eventual fate, and there is no reason to believe he ever revisited his birthplace of East Looe. It is possible that he returned to the East Indies and to his homosexual lover, John Swann, or to New York, a place known to him, and friendly to pirates. Being homosexual, it is unlikely that he left any descendants, so unless some chance record of him is found in old documents, what finally happened to him will remain unknown.

There being severall prisoners in the
Marshalsea, who were comitted there for Pyracy, and having lain
there some time, I understood it was the Lords pleasure to have a
day fix't for the appointment of an Admiralty Sessions to be held
for their Tryall, and in order to it I have waited on Dr Oxenden
about setling the same. I find he is of opinion that munday the
19th of January will be a very convenient day to begin it, if I can by
that time be ready with the evidence, that are to prove the facts for
which the prisoners are to be Indicted, but in regard our most
material witness against the chiefest of them Capt Burgess, is
Robert Collover a prisoner in Newgate under a conviction of
Pyracy, I beg leave to remind their Lordships of the case that was
laid before them abt 10 days since signed by Dr Newton & Mr Lechmere
relating to his pardon; There are two things in it to induce his
majesty to grant it; and the first is, his voluntary Submission upon
receiving the proclamation that promised it; and the other of the
readiness he now shews of doing very considerable Service in being
instrumental by his evidence in convicting those, he knows have
been guilty of those crimes; tis this last reason, makes me thus Solicitous
to obtain it; and indeed so little proof is there at present agt Burgess
that there is no probability of convicting him without it. Tis therefore
my humble opinion, that it wont be proper to appoint a day for a
Sessions, till his majesties pleasure is known in this matter. The prisoners
now in custody have been there severall months, and having been no
Sessions held since may last, I believe their Lordships will think
it convenient to order one as soon as may be. but since by this
mans pardon wee shall be able to make the proof appear more
fully against them; I desire you will be pleased to lay the same
before their Lordships, and acquaint them this is the first step is
necessary to be made, towards holding of a Sessions, and am

Sr
your most humble Servant
Decembr 9. 1701
Tho Bale

Thomas Bale's Letter

References

The Bishop's Transcripts, St Martin's by Looe.
County Records Office, Truro, Cornwall.

Documents from the Public Records Office, Kew, London.

Royal Geographical Society, 1 Kensington Gore, London

'The Wordsworth Dictionary of Pirates' by Jan Rogozínski.
Published by Wordsworth Editions Limited.

'Captain Kidd and the War Against the Pirates' by R.C. Ritchie.
Published by Harvard University Press.

'The Trials of Captain Kidd' by Graham Brook.
Published by William Hodge and Company Limited.

'No Purchase No Pay'. A Winston Publication,
Eyre and Spottiswoode.

'Pirates of the Eastern Seas' by Charles Grey.

The Authors

Published by Carrack Widn
Quay Cottage, The Quay, East Looe
Cornwall. PL13 1AQ

Research by Gendall/Raddy
Text by J. E. Gendall
Introduction by R. Raddy/J. E. Gendall
Photography (uncredited) by R. Raddy
Design and illustrations by K. Raddy

ISBN: 0-9540602-0-2

Anne the daughter of Mr Nathaniel Drumpton & Mrs Elizabeth baptised January [illegible]

John the son of Richard Colling & Jane baptised february [illegible] 166[illegible]

Joane the daughter of Richard Kindome & wilmoth baptised febr: [illegible] 166[illegible]

Denny the son of Richard [illegible] & Mary baptised february the viij 166[illegible]

Phineas the Son of Philip Jordan & Mary baptised March [illegible]

Walter ye son of Danyel Burt & Jane baptised March [illegible]

Marjory the daughter of John [illegible] baptised March [illegible]

Robert the son of Pasko Colliver & Anne baptised March the viijth — 1665

Henry the son of William Watkins & Edith baptised march the viij — 1665

Peter Evens the son of Peter Evens & Edith baptised April the xxiij 1666

Thomas the son of John Dominy & Agnes baptised May 1st 166[illegible]

Dorothy the daughter of Richard Pope & Marjory baptised May vijth 166[illegible]

Joane the daughter of Jeffery Moorshead & Jane baptised June vth 166[illegible]

Rupert the son of William Saunderrocke & Thamosin baptised June [illegible] 166[illegible]

Joane the daughter of John Kendu & Katharine baptised June [illegible] 166[illegible]

[illegible] the son of Ferdinando Hearle & Elizabeth baptised June [illegible] 166[illegible]

The Baptismal record of Robert Colliver.